why it works

Materials

QEB Publishing

Author Anna Claybourne
Consultant Terry Jennings
Editor Louisa Somerville
Designer Susi Martin
Picture Researcher Claudia Tate
Illustrator John Haslam

Publisher Steve Evans
Creative Director Zeta Davies

Library of Congress Control Number: 2008011711

ISBN 978 1 59566 557 7

Printed and bound in China

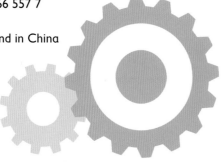

Words in **bold** can be
found in the glossary
on page 22.

Contents

Stuff everywhere!

Look around you. What can you see? Everywhere you look, there are materials!

Things people have made, such as chairs, bicycles, and books, are made of materials. So are natural things such as rocks, trees, water, and your body.

Plastic

Wood

Look at the objects in this classroom. They are all made of materials.

4

There are lots of different types of materials, such as wood, glass, wool, and plastic.

Wool

Glass

It's a fact

A material is anything that takes up space. You can usually feel a material or touch it.

5

How does it feel?

Materials feel different from each other. For example, they might feel rough or smooth, hard or soft.

Try this

This guessing game lets you feel lots of materials.

Cork

1 Put on a blindfold. Ask an adult to put objects made of different materials onto a tray.

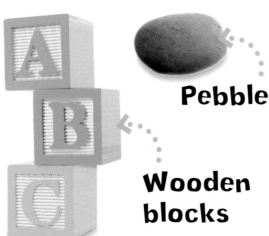

Pebble

Wooden blocks

2 Feel the objects with your hands. Are they smooth or rough, soft or hard, dry or slippery, warm or cold? Can you tell what they are?

Tissue paper

Ball of wool

Pieces of chocolate

Piece of cheese

Cotton wool

Seashell

Metal coin

Eraser

Plastic spoon

A metal coin feels hard and cold. You cannot squash it.

Cotton wool feels soft and warm. It's easy to squash.

Where are materials from?

We get materials from all kinds of places to make the things we need. Materials are made from animals or plants, or come from the Earth.

Try this

You need a pile of different materials.

Try to sort the materials into three piles.

Cheese

Wool

1. Things that come from an animal.

Wool comes from sheep. Cheese is usually made from cows' milk. Seashells are made by sea creatures.

Seashell

2. Things that come from plants.

Paper is made from wood. Wood comes from trees. Cotton also comes from plants.

Paper

Wood

Cotton wool

3. Things that come from the Earth.

Rocks and metals come from the Earth. These materials are known as minerals.

Metal coin

Pebble

MATERIALS WE MAKE

Some materials are made by people from natural things. Glass is made from sand, and plastic is made from oil, from the Earth.

Some materials belong in more than one pile! Chocolate contains milk from an animal and cocoa from a plant.

Chocolate

9

How hard?

Some materials are soft, others hard. You can test them to find out how hard or soft they are.

Try this

You need objects made of different materials, such as:

★ **rubber ball**
★ **pebble**
★ **cotton wool ball**
★ **seashell**
★ **cork**
★ **sock**
★ **grape**
★ **piece of modeling clay**

1 Test the objects to see how hard they are. Try squeezing them, bending them, or tapping them with a spoon. Hard materials do not change their shape. Soft ones do change shape.

Socks

Pebble

Modeling clay

Seashell

2 Make a list of the objects. Make the hardest material number 1. Make the next hardest number 2, and so on.

3 Ask your friends or family to try it too. Do you all agree which things are hardest? Some materials, such as stone and shell, may feel equally hard.

Cork

Grapes

Cotton wool

HARDEST
1. pebble

Sink or float?

Metal coin

When you put a material in water, it will either float or sink.

Here is another test to try on materials.

Try this

You need a bowl of water and a few objects.

Here are some ideas for materials to try:

★ **metal coin**
★ **cork**
★ **modeling clay**
★ **plastic toy figure**
★ **pebble**
★ **wooden block**
★ **wax crayon**
★ **polystyrene foam**

Pebble

Wax crayons

Cork

Wooden block

TESTING, TESTING!

Scientists often do tests like this on materials. They find out how materials work, and what they are useful for.

Place the objects in the bowl. Which ones float and which ones sink?

Can you think of what things that float are useful for? What about things that sink?

Plastic toy

This life jacket is made of a kind of foam that floats easily.

Strength test

This experiment lets you see how strong materials are. You could test printer paper, tissue paper, and kitchen foil.

Try this

You need a small and a large yogurt pot, a rubber band, and some marbles. The marbles should all be the same size.

1 Lay a piece of printer paper over the large yogurt pot. Use a rubber band to hold it in place.

2 Stand the smaller yogurt pot on top of the printer paper.

3 Put marbles into the pot one by one, until the paper tears and the pot falls down.

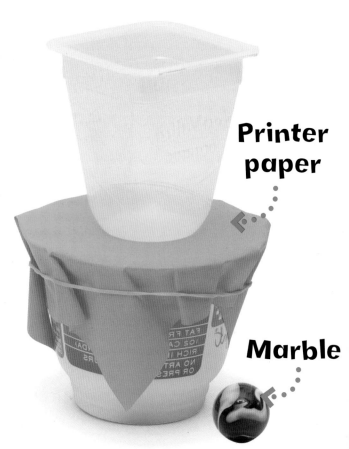

Printer paper

Marble

Do the same test with the other materials. Which one holds up the most marbles before it breaks?

Can you think of other tests you could do? How would you test if a material was waterproof?

How would you test for bendiness or stretchiness?

Kitchen foil

Tissue paper

Yogurt pot

The right material?

Objects are made from materials that suit the job they have to do.

Can you think why a cooking spoon is made of wood?

It does not get hot easily, so its handle stays cool.

It has no taste, so it won't spoil the food.

It won't break if you drop it.

It's a fact
Wood does not melt when it gets hot.

These jeans are made from tough cotton **fabric**. Why?

Cotton bends with you when you move.

It feels soft and keeps you warm. It's easy to wash and dry.

It's important to choose the right material for the job. What if things were made from the wrong materials?

WRONG MATERIALS!

What would happen if a wooden spoon was made of cloth? What if your jeans were made of wood?

Solid or liquid?

You have tested **solid** objects, such as coins, spoons, and corks. **Liquids** are materials, too. Water is a material. So are milk, juice, and all other liquids.

What's the difference between a solid and a liquid? Try these tests on a small beaker of water and some uncooked pasta.

Try this

What happens if you try to pour the water and the pasta onto a plate?

Can you push your finger into the water and the pasta?

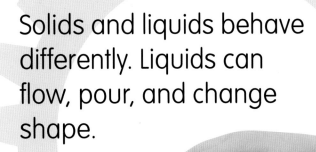

Solids and liquids behave differently. Liquids can flow, pour, and change shape.

Solids keep their shape.

There is another type of material too. It is called a **gas**. Gases spread out everywhere and are usually hard to see. The air is made of gases.

Can you pour the water and the pasta through a sieve?

It's a fact

A material can be a solid, a liquid, or a gas.

Changing materials

Materials can change between solids, liquids, and gases. Usually, getting hotter or colder makes them change.

Have you ever seen someone put a lump of butter into a hot pan? What happens?

The solid butter melts. It changes into a liquid.

Try this:

You need two plastic beakers with a little water in them. Make sure you put the same amount in each beaker.

1 Put one beaker of water into the freezer.

2 Put the other beaker on a warm heater or on a sunny windowsill. Leave overnight.

Frozen beaker **Sun-warmed beaker**

It's a fact

The water in the freezer has changed into ice. It has changed from a liquid into a solid.

The water left in a warm place has gone! It has changed into a gas and floated away.

When water is boiled, it turns into a gas called steam.

MORE CHANGES

Can you think of other material changes? What happens to chocolate when you put it in your mouth? What happens to an ice cream in the Sun?

21

Glossary

Fabric

Cloth, made of cotton or wool for example. Cloth is often used for making clothes.

Gas

A type of material. Gas spreads out to fill the space it is in.

Liquid

A type of material, such as water, milk, oil, or vinegar, that can flow and be poured.

Material

What objects are made from. A table is made from wood and a window from glass. Wood and glass are materials.

Melt

When a solid, such as butter, ice, or chocolate, turns to liquid as it is warmed.

Mineral

A type of material that comes from the Earth.

Solid

A type of material that has a fixed shape and holds together.

Test

An experiment that helps you to find out about something.

Index

Notes for parents and teachers

• Encourage children to look out for as many materials as possible in everyday life. Point out interesting and unusual materials such as carbon fiber and joke putty, and talk about what they might be made of and how they work. You could help children to look them up in books or on the Internet to find out more about them.

•There are many more materials tests that children can experiment with. Try designing experiments to test whether materials are attracted by a magnet, to find out how well they conduct heat, or how bendy or elastic they are. Encourage children to record their results on paper.

• Discuss why objects are made of the materials they are and how this helps them to do their jobs. Often, different parts of an object are made from different materials. Point out things like a vegetable peeler with a rubber handle, or the metal eyelets in shoes to hold the laces—why are they there?

• Sometimes objects don't do their jobs well. For example, plastic toys break and jeans wear through at the knees. Encourage children to think up ways to design better objects, or invent new ones to do the job better. Ask them to draw their designs and inventions with labels for the materials they would use.

• Same objects can be made of different materials: spoons can be metal, wood, or plastic; bags can be plastic, fabric, or leather. What are the advantages of different materials and how can they be put to different uses?

•Look for different states of matter in everyday life. Liquids include cooking oils, fuel and saliva; gases include domestic cooking gas and camping gas; there are gases in your breath.

• Point out changes of state in everyday life, such as water freezing and melting in different weather conditions, clothes drying on the washing line, and food melting and hardening during cooking.